Pfeiffer™

Creative Style Profile

Beverly Kaye and Beverly Olevin

BICENTENNIAL
1807
WILEY
2007
BICENTENNIAL

John Wiley & Sons, Inc.

ISBN-10: 0-7879-8966-5
ISBN-13: 978-0-7879-8966-8

Acquiring Editor: Martin Delahoussaye
Director of Development: Kathleen Dolan Davies
Developmental Editor: Susan Rachmeler
Production Editor: Dawn Kilgore
Editor: Rebecca Taff
Manufacturing Supervisor: Becky Carreño
Design, composition, technical art: Leigh McLellan Design

Printed in the United States of America
Printing   10   9   8   7   6   5   4

Contents

Introduction *v*

Creative Style Profile *1*

Scoring Sheet *5*

The Five Creative Styles *7*

Working Creatively with Others *15*

Creative Style Combinations *17*

What Now? *23*

Introduction

*You can train yourself to think more creatively. Creativity is not just
a talent some people are born with. Working creatively can make you
more productive and motivated.*

Most of us spent long school years training ourselves to think logically. We have succeeded masterfully. But what have we lost? Our curious mind, our endless imagination, our joy of discovery—are these lost forever? We had all these things as children. We need to relearn them as adults.

Creative thinking doesn't belong only to the painter, the musician, the dancer, or the inventor. Creative thinking increases productivity in everyone: the manager, the engineer, the secretary, the teacher, and the government administrator. And it can increase the satisfaction and excitement in our work.

We are all creative. We just express that creativity in different ways. All of us can become more creative once we are aware of our own unique strengths and abilities. This awareness is a powerful tool in selecting and developing careers that will bring out the best in us.

The Creative Style Profile is designed not to tell you WHETHER you are creative, but HOW you are creative. It is *not* a test of creativity, but an exploration of where your creative strengths lie.

The questionnaire will help you discover how your individual creativity expresses itself. Please read through the instructions before proceeding. And remember, there are no "right" answers—just the right answers for *you.*

Creative Style Profile

Instructions: Read and then rate each of the thirty-five statements on a scale of 1 to 6 to indicate to what extent the statement is true for you. Circle the appropriate number next to each statement.

Think of yourself primarily in a work environment. Answer in terms of what you believe or know to be true about yourself.

When you finish, transfer your results to the Scoring Sheet that follows the inventory, and total your results for each style.

Rating Scale

1	2	3	4	5	6
Never	Rarely	Occasionally	Frequently	Almost Always	Always

1. I notice one thing and think how it applies to something totally different.	1	2	3	4	5	6
2. My thoughts often float to loosely formed ideas.	1	2	3	4	5	6
3. I crave making new opportunities happen.	1	2	3	4	5	6
4. I can take an abstract plan and build it into a working physical model.	1	2	3	4	5	6
5. Curiosity pushes me to spend intense hours following trails to see where they might lead.	1	2	3	4	5	6
6. My wit and humor provide me with different ways of looking at things.	1	2	3	4	5	6
7. When I wake, I remember impressions and visions from my dreams that inspire ideas.	1	2	3	4	5	6
8. I enjoy playing the leading or controlling role in a project.	1	2	3	4	5	6
9. I think about a problem, then picture how it will be solved.	1	2	3	4	5	6
10. I enjoy the challenge of experimentation in unknown areas.	1	2	3	4	5	6

1	2	3	4	5	6
Never	**Rarely**	**Occasionally**	**Frequently**	**Almost Always**	**Always**

11. I like playing with words and phrases, for
    example, puns.   1 2 3 4 5 6

12. As I work, I don't think about the final results.   1 2 3 4 5 6

13. I actively seek the excitement of change.   1 2 3 4 5 6

14. Mental imagery helps me envision things
    I plan to construct.   1 2 3 4 5 6

15. My mental concentration is so intense when
    I am investigating an idea that I don't stop for
    breaks or even to eat.   1 2 3 4 5 6

16. I am a good observer of the physical world.   1 2 3 4 5 6

17. Thoughts and images jump around in my head
    without my knowing where they will lead me.   1 2 3 4 5 6

18. I am good at influencing others.   1 2 3 4 5 6

19. My hands are quicker than my mind in
    discovering new ways of doing things.   1 2 3 4 5 6

20. Solutions to problems come to me when I am
    asking myself questions rather than looking
    for answers.   1 2 3 4 5 6

21. I have patience with ambiguity when the best
    option is not yet clear.   1 2 3 4 5 6

22. Solutions to problems come to me suddenly,
    with great clarity, as if from nowhere.   1 2 3 4 5 6

23. I like pushing myself to work at the edge of my
    competence.   1 2 3 4 5 6

24. Ideas come to me when I am working with
    physical materials, object, textures, colors,
    and shapes.   1 2 3 4 5 6

25. I have patience with work that takes me down
    blind alleys because eventually there may be a
    breakthrough.   1 2 3 4 5 6

26. Solutions to problems come to me when I see
    the connections between things that I never
    saw before.   1 2 3 4 5 6

27. When an idea comes to me, I don't think first
    about whether it will work.   1 2 3 4 5 6

1	2	3	4	5	6
Never	Rarely	Occasionally	Frequently	Almost Always	Always

28. Ideas become exciting to me when I see how
    I can turn them into successful products or
    programs.   1   2   3   4   5   6

29. I can visualize the way I want things to be.   1   2   3   4   5   6

30. Once an idea, a theoretical possibility, comes
    to me, I am driven to explore it, even if it means
    a great deal of research.   1   2   3   4   5   6

31. I see things in new ways by using analogies,
    metaphors, and similes.   1   2   3   4   5   6

32. I can be absent-minded, forgetting practical
    things that should be done.   1   2   3   4   5   6

33. I enjoy the challenge of bringing together the
    energy, people, and resources that will make
    an idea happen.   1   2   3   4   5   6

34. Solutions to problems come to me when I can
    physically work with objects and materials.   1   2   3   4   5   6

35. I enjoy probing into the underlying issues of a
    problem because there is always more to know
    than what meets the eye.   1   2   3   4   5   6

Scoring Sheet

Instructions: Transfer your ratings from the Profile onto the appropriate line below and then add the numbers in each column. The column with the highest number is your dominant style. If your two highest scores are within two points of each other, then both styles can be considered dominant. In that case, you'll find the section on creative style combinations on the next pages of particular interest.

Connector	Dreamer	Innovator	Builder	Explorer
1 _____	2 _____	3 _____	4 _____	5 _____
6 _____	7 _____	8 _____	9 _____	10 _____
11 _____	12 _____	13 _____	14 _____	15 _____
16 _____	17 _____	18 _____	19 _____	20 _____
21 _____	22 _____	23 _____	24 _____	25 _____
26 _____	27 _____	28 _____	29 _____	30 _____
31 _____	32 _____	33 _____	34 _____	35 _____
Total _____	Total _____	Total _____	Total _____	Total _____

The Five Creative Styles

What do your answers tell you about *how* you are creative?

On the following pages, you'll find descriptions of each of the five creative styles. In addition to learning about your own style, read about the other styles, which will help you to better understand how you might expand your creativity, as well as how to collaborate with people with different styles.

Connector

Perspective: **Perceptive-Oriented**

> *"An idea is a feat of association."*
> —*Robert Frost, Poet*

The Connector's creativity is based on the ability to see relationships between previously unrelated things. This requires a high degree of flexibility and an openness to all possibilities.

Connectors' minds function a bit like the random access memory (RAM) of a computer. They have a large stored memory, which can be quickly accessed to respond to a problem. Their memories can jump from one reference to another without the need for a linear sequence. Connectors are good observers. They take in information from many sources constantly. They don't judge the value or the application immediately. The creative applications may come down the road.

People who score highest in Connector excel at lateral thinking, as opposed to traditional linear thinking. When confronted with a problem, they can use analogies and metaphors to see a situation in a new way. Connectors are often able to see the humor in difficult situations. They are good problem solvers and brainstormers. They can bring fresh approaches to chronic problems.

Flexibility with words, phrases, and thoughts allows Connectors to play with alternative ideas. This play generates the abstract connections. This stream-of-consciousness thinking can be exciting for other people to interact with as they search for ways to solve their own problems. Connectors may be able to refine key elements of situations quickly and synthesize creative solutions.

Connectors often search for the best answers, not necessarily the right answers, and in so doing are able to produce unexpected and spontaneous ideas.

Strengths

- Observant
- Spontaneous
- Witty/humorous
- Light-hearted
- Flexible
- Open
- Non-sequential
- Playful

Insights

- You may be seen as frivolous or distracting when you move others away from their direct focus, so be sensitive to the frustrations of others.
- Your lateral thinking skills may be misunderstood or intimidating to others. You need to frequently check that others are tracking your thinking processes and are staying with you.
- When others discard new ideas as impractical or unrealistic, look for how a key component in that idea may have another application.
- As your mind wanders in the consideration of a problem, work to merge different frames of reference until they collide into a new approach.

Questions to Ponder

- If this is your highest-scoring creative style, how can you use these insights to help develop your career?
- If this is one of your lowest scores, consider whether there is any benefit in increasing your strengths in this style. Look back at the inventory and see whether there is one behavior that you might want to work on improving over the next six months.

"It seems so obvious once the connection has been made, yet in great inventions the joined matrices were initially far apart, belonging to different realms, like electricity and magnetism, before electromagnetism."
—Arthur Koestler, Philosopher

Dreamer

Perspective: **Receptive-Oriented**

> *"The germ of a future composition comes suddenly and unexpectedly. It takes root with extraordinary force. I thought out the scherzo of our symphony—the moment of its composition—exactly as you heard it."*
> *—Peter Tchaikovsky, Composer*

The Dreamer's creativity is most dramatically characterized by the breakthrough of ideas from below the level of conscious awareness. Dreamers frequently get impressions, ideas, and visions as if from nowhere. Their creative strength lies in the ability to tap into these visions and to *"see"* without needing to understand or organize. They are not looking at the whole or final outcome. All of their ideas are initially valid because Dreamers are non-judgmental. They react more from their instincts.

People who score highest in Dreamer are not usually goal-driven, so they can relax and be receptive to images and ideas. Dreamers' ideas may be described as coming from "out of the blue" or "suddenly dawning on me."

Dreamers are the people we most frequently think of when we are asked to describe "creative behaviors." Their intelligence is most in touch with Carl Jung's concept of the "collective unconscious." They have vivid imaginations, and when their ideas are realized, their work seems to reveal a universal truth. Dreamers reflect the images and experiences shared by all peoples of the world. They can be visionaries with often uncanny insights, born from "free-form" creativity.

People who have worked on a problem unsuccessfully for a long time often find solutions and breakthroughs when they forget about the problem and think about something else. Solutions come suddenly and with great clarity while they're in the shower or out jogging. It is in this moment that they are most in touch with their Dreamers' creative intelligence.

Strengths

- Instinctual
- Relaxed
- Patient
- Vivid imagination
- Insightful
- Fanciful
- Non-judgmental
- Free-form thinker

Insights

- Your ideas may be seen by others as impractical or unrealistic and can be easily squelched by others. Find non-judgmental people whom you trust to share your visions and incomplete ideas with.

- Don't let go of your vision just because you see no clear path of implementation. Push yourself to develop your impressions and instincts.

- Respect your insights and trust yourself to put them forward with confidence.

- Collaborate with Innovators and Connectors. They will help you focus your ideas into realistic outcomes.

Questions to Ponder

- If this is your highest-scoring creative style, how can you use these insights to help develop your career?

- If this is one of your lowest scores, consider whether there is any benefit in increasing your strengths in this style. Look back at the inventory and see whether there is one behavior that you might want to work on improving over the next six months.

Innovator

Perspective: **Goal-Oriented**

> *"Like most great ideas, it came from something that was right in front of us. We designed this computer because we couldn't afford to buy one. We got started with nothing, just nothing!"*
> —Steve Jobs, Entrepreneur

"The root from which all knowledge grows lies in the ability to draw conclusions from what we see to what we do not see; to move our minds through space and time; and to recognize ourselves in the past on the steps to the present."
—Jacob Bronowski, **The Ascent of Man**

The Innovator's creativity springs from a concept of the future and the intense desire to control that future. Innovators want to understand what is possible and then to act on this understanding. This creative intelligence is based on the way they see things in final form and as finished products.

People who score highest in Innovator are very entrepreneurial in character, embracing and generating change. Growth and change are driving forces for Innovators. They are constantly open to new opportunities, which may come from ideas generated by themselves or others. But ultimately it is the Innovators who manage the execution of those ideas. They do this by energizing and motivating others. They are magnetic people who take the lead and exert influence. They bring high energy and contagious enthusiasm to their work.

Innovators frequently operate at the edge of their knowledge and competence, focusing their attention and resources in new areas. They are risk-takers because they venture into new areas, but the constant control they have over every step in the process reduces the danger to acceptable risks. Speculation is ever-present in the Innovator's mind. They are bottom-line oriented, and new ideas are acted on quickly and decisively.

Ultimately, Innovators are adaptive to change. Their creative process begins with the constant search for new concepts and ideas. They activate and coordinate necessary resources to launch a project. Their work culminates in something that did not exist before. Their unique ability is to recognize a vacuum and then to fill it creatively.

Strengths

- Motivated

- Enjoys change

- Organized

- Decisive

- Takes charge

- Influential

- Adaptable

- Entrepreneurial

Insights

- You may make decisions without considering the perspectives of others, thereby closing your mind too early and limiting your alternatives.

- Ask for and listen to the thoughts and ideas of others. Even if those thoughts don't immediately fit with your ultimate goal, have patience with ambiguity.

- As an Innovator, you are in the strongest position to bring together the strengths of other people. Balance your staff and task forces to make the most effective use of all the creative intelligences.

- Trust your competitive instincts and your own competencies.

Questions to Ponder

- If this is your highest-scoring creative style, how can you use these insights to help develop your career?

- If this is one of your lowest scores, consider whether there is any benefit in increasing your strengths in this style. Look back at the inventory and see whether there is one behavior that you might want to work on improving over the next six months.

Builder

Perspective: **Visually Oriented**

> *"I get the solid shape, as it were, inside my head. I identify*
> *myself with the center of its gravity, its mass, its weight . . .*
> *imagine it any size I like and really am in control, almost*
> *like God creating something."*
> —Henry Moore, Sculptor

The Builder's creativity is expressed in the actual construction and final physical representation of his or her ideas. The essence of this creative intelligence is the Builder's ability to visualize how materials come together as the work evolves. Builders may not intellectualize new concepts but experience them as they happen.

Once an idea is generated, Builders can become very detail-oriented. They are dedicated to making things work as perfectly as possible. They can become totally absorbed in watching their creation grow. The initial concept may be their own, or they may take ideas begun by others and build on them until they are realized.

Builders are involved in actual physical hands-on work. They may have specific tools related to their means of expression. In fact, Builders may turn to their tools to give them ideas in solving a problem or moving beyond an impasse.

People who score highest in Builder are quite visual. They are highly aware of texture, shape, color, space, mass, and weight. These provide them with an abundance of ideas and alternatives. Their trial-and-error approach can result in new, creative ways of seeing things.

Builders often picture clearly, in their mind's eyes, the challenges ahead and how they will confront them. Although they may have a vision of the desired results, they are not limited by that vision. The final outcome of their work is certainly satisfying, but the real pleasure comes from the building process itself.

"Building fun into business is vital. We should not relegate it to something we buy after work with money we earn."
—Michael Phillips

Strengths

- Artistic
- Detailed
- Resourceful
- Focused
- Ingenious
- Adept with hands
- Inventive

Insights

- Your need for making your work as perfect as possible may keep you focused on small details while missing the big picture.

- Your total absorption in the process of creating may concern others if they don't feel you have a reliable timetable for project completion. Practice good time management so that pressure doesn't build up and hinder the free flow of your ideas.

- Trust your visual sense of what works and what doesn't. Learn to describe your ideas to others so that they can see them as you do.

- Enjoy playing with the materials of your work. Collaborate with a Connector, who can add humor and alternative combinations.

Questions to Ponder

- If this is your highest-scoring creative style, how can you use these insights to help develop your career?

- If this is one of your lowest scores, consider whether there is any benefit in increasing your strengths in this style. Look back at the inventory and see whether there is one behavior that you might want to work on improving over the next six months.

Explorer

Perspective: **Action-Oriented**

> *"I roamed the countryside searching for answers to things I did not understand. Why shells existed on the tops of mountains. . . why a bird sustains itself in the air. These questions and other strange phenomena engaged my thought throughout my life."*
> —Leonardo da Vinci, Renaissance Man

The Explorer's creativity emanates from the energy for challenge and adventure. Curiosity is the driving force that pushes Explorers to go beyond existing knowledge to unknown frontiers. Their creative intelligence can be focused, patient, and analytical. They will follow experimental trails in the search for new ground.

Explorers are able to free themselves from conventional and established standards. Their fascination with the exploratory process pushes them to take risks, even when there is a strong possibility of failure. They often do fail, but are able to learn from these experiences and move on. When they do succeed, real breakthroughs can be the result.

People who score highest in Explorer are action-oriented, usually preferring "doing" to "discussing." They may retreat from extensive social involvement, choosing instead to work alone or with a few close colleagues. Preoccupation with the pursuit of their tasks gives them little tolerance for people distractions.

Explorers look for the right questions that they should be asking themselves in the discovery phase of their work. The asking of difficult theoretical questions and the posing of hypothetical situations leads them to thought processes that avoid traditional, logical thinking. The work itself reveals paths to follow. These methods combine to promote the constant challenging of limits.

Strengths

- Adventurous
- Risk taker
- Unconventional
- Investigative
- Analytical
- Not socially driven
- Challenge limits

> *"Without playing with fantasy, no creative work has ever yet come to birth."*
> —Carl Jung

Insights

- Your single-focused energy may keep you from taking advantage of unexpected opportunities. Don't miss a new track that might be more productive than the one you're on.

- Share your ideas with others, even if their experience and discipline are different from your own. They may offer you a fresh perspective.

- Pick challenges that really excite you so that you will be motivated to see difficult dilemmas through to their resolutions.

- Value your need for autonomy and independence. Help others appreciate that your best creative work happens when these elements are present.

Questions to Ponder

- If this is your highest-scoring creative style, how can you use these insights to help develop your career?

- If this is one of your lowest scores, consider whether there is any benefit in increasing your strengths in this style. Look back at the inventory and see whether there is one behavior that you might want to work on improving over the next six months.

Working Creatively with Others

The Creative Style Profile helps you look at your own creative skills and strengths. Now you need to determine who the best people are for you to collaborate with. Combining different creative styles and strengths can lead to heightened creative thinking, work excitement, and individual as well as group productivity.

Consider the creative styles of the people you work with (employees, colleagues, and supervisors). Use the grid below to track the style composition of your team. Insert member names across the top and check off the appropriate style for each person. This grid can then serve as a quick reference during teamwork or discussions.

Members / Styles							
Connector							
Dreamer							
Innovator							
Builder							
Explorer							

Creative Style Combinations

Style combinations can be interpreted in two ways:

1. *For the individual:* Find the combination that matches your two highest style scores. Read about how each strength can support the other.

2. *For dyads or teams:* Find the combination that matches you and a colleague or team members. Read about how your strengths complement one another. Or read each of the entries that contains your dominant style to better understand how to collaborate with others.

Note: The descriptions are written for the individual, but apply equally well to dyads and teams.

Innovator/Connector

Goal-Oriented and Perceptive-Oriented

This combination makes for a particularly strong leader. Not only are they open to new ideas, they have what it takes to summon the resources to make the ideas happen. As managers they listen to what their people have to say and observe all that's going on between the lines. The Innovator's strengths that drive them to control projects and move them forward quickly are tempered by the Connector's strengths of accumulating and evaluating relevant information over a long period of time. The lateral thinking skills and sense of humor of a Connector that can often frustrate colleagues are tempered by the Innovator's continual need to stay on track.

> *"I like to have a good time with my staff, even though I drive everybody crazy with all my humor. They probably tolerate it because they know I can really charge them up when there is an opportunity to make new things happen around here."*

Innovator/Dreamer

Goal-Oriented and Receptive-Oriented

This is a rare combination, really a contradiction. Since the Innovator is goal-oriented and the Dreamer is not, it seems that these creative behaviors could not exist in the same personality. But the essence of creative thinking is the ability to live with inconsistencies, for ultimately, inconsistencies produce the most original thoughts. The Dreamer's non-directive and non-judgmental perspective moderates the Innovator's rush toward immediate resolution.

> *"Sometimes I feel schizophrenic–I'm off in the clouds and can't seem to ground myself, then suddenly everything clicks and I know exactly what I need to do and I can't wait to do it."*

Connector/Builder

Perceptive-Oriented and Visual-Oriented

This combination can produce some fresh and unconventional visions. The Builder's tendency to engage in intense, focused work can be productively enhanced by the Connector's infusion of divergent ideas. The Connector serves as a catalyst to move the Builder through a multitude of permutations and possibilities.

> *"I had the greatest version of a new toy for my kids, putting together my '50s toys with space age technology. I didn't really know how I'd do it, till I went into my workshop and started physically playing with all the stuff."*

Builder/Explorer

Visual-Oriented and Action-Oriented

This combination may indicate a person who is somewhat of a loner. His or her world is filled with the excitement and process of discovery. These two styles within one person complement one another closely. The result is a strong capability to invent. The Builder benefits by the Explorer's dedicated investigation of *how* things work. The Explorer is enhanced by the Builder's ability to *make* things work.

> *"Ever since I was a kid, I've loved putting things together—model airplanes and those great sailing ships. Now that I'm an engineer, I still do the same thing and love it even more. Because there's always new research and more to learn, I can take my visions even farther."*

Innovator/Explorer

Goal-Oriented and Action-Oriented

This combination produces a very dynamic personality. People with this combination are often intensely excited and challenged by their work. The Explorer's patient investigation contributes to the illumination phase of the creative process. The Innovator takes these discoveries to the next step, turning them into fully implemented products and services.

> *"I've been working on this project for almost a year now, and am sad to see the research stage end. We're moving into piloting the system next month. So I'm shifting gears and looking forward to putting my new team together."*

> **"Every child is an artist. The problem is how to remain an artist once he grows up."**
> **—Pablo Picasso**

Connector/Explorer

Perceptive-Oriented and Action-Oriented

This combination can lead to original scientific thinking. The Explorer is frequently in the process of researching, accumulating, and assimilating information. With the Connector's perspective, all this information can be retrieved in lateral as well as linear ways. The Explorer's insights will be greatly enhanced by the Connector's bisociative thinking (the ability to connect things that previously had no connection whatsoever).

> *"I'd been sitting at my computer for days trying to design a new program, and felt I was at a dead end. Then I started thinking about the USC/UCLA football game and remembered an ingenious play. Slowly, I saw how I could use a similar sequence to make my program work."*

Innovator/Builder

Goal-Oriented and Visual-Oriented

This combination can be the profile of a successful creator. Not only do these people have the skills to create beauty and function with their hands, but they have the ability to promote their work in the marketplace. The Innovator's enthusiasm keeps the Builder from losing himself or herself in the details of the work and forgetting the excitement of the original vision. As the Builder works, the process is enhanced by the

Innovator's need to look for new ways to put things together. This combination strives for changes in traditional focus and patterns.

> *"Sometimes in my work as a graphic artist it seems that my clients are asking for the same kinds of things. I love to surprise them by changing things around completely. My greatest kick is when I take a real risk and it works."*

Explorer/Dreamer

Action-Oriented and Receptive-Oriented

This combination produces some of the most important skills in the entire creative process. The Dreamer brings imagination and a real visionary perspective to the Explorer's very specific and analytical work. The Dreamer's nonjudgmental approach can intercede at any point in the Explorer's work; the Dreamer may provide the initial vision that moves the Explorer to action, loosens the process along the way, and finally gives the sudden illumination that makes everything work.

> *"Last year when I was put in charge of that preliminary design project, I had one wild idea after another. I was having a ball, even though everybody thought I was nuts. I guess they were really surprised when, after three months of obsessive exploration of my best idea, it really turned out to be the answer."*

Connector/Dreamer

Perceptive-Oriented and Receptive-Oriented

This combination can be both lighthearted and deeply introspective. The Dreamer's wealth of loosely defined images can be enlarged and transformed by the Connector. The stream-of-consciousness possibilities in this combination are endless. The Connector's ability to see how previously unconnected things might relate in a new way is greatly enhanced by the multitude of colorful images from the Dreamer's vivid imagination.

"I discovered the Theory of Relativity by picturing myself riding on a ray of light."
—Albert Einstein

> *"My mind was totally unfocused as I watched the rain fall gently on the windowpane. The drops moved across the pane instead of straight down. I realized how we could re-route the work flow to make things so much simpler and more efficient in my department."*

Dreamer/Builder

Receptive-Oriented and Visual-Oriented

This combination can be the most artistic of all the creative combinations. Visions and ideas come to this person from both external and internal sources. The visions play on one another until reality and fantasy are almost indistinguishable. The sculptor or painter whose work reveals universal truth seems to speak to everyone, even if they can't intellectually understand its power. The Dreamer's vivid imagination finds the skill for actual physical expression in the Builder.

> *"I had a real clear vision of how I wanted to remodel my house,*
> *but every time I looked at the plans I had dreams of people moving*
> *through the space in slow motion. What could this mean? I woke in*
> *the middle of the night and realized the beams were too heavy for the*
> *slope of the ceiling and it gave the feeling of weight and oppression."*

What Now?

This workshop should be only the beginning of your creative journey. Here are some key questions for you to think about in the weeks and months ahead.

Questions to Ponder

- What other perspectives would enhance and support my way of doing things?

- Who are the people I can share my ideas with easily? Who can I trust to listen without being judgmental?

- How might my creative intelligence be stepped on or limited by the behaviors of others? What do I need to do to prevent this?

- What are the creative styles of the people I really admire? What can I learn from them to develop additional strengths and increase my creativity in other ways?

Questions to Consider If You Manage Others

- What are the creative styles of my key employees?

- What are the things I need to be thinking about if I manage others? How can I build a balance in my work team so that all perspectives are represented? How do the different creative styles of my team interact?

- How can knowing my employees' creative strengths help me to better coach them in developing their careers?

- How might I coach employees with styles different from my own?

- What conflicts can occur when my employees and I have different styles? How might this impact their careers?

- What specific things can I do to make the environment more conducive to creativity for my team?

- How will these changes impact my employees' productivity?